The Great Smoky Mountains

CRESCENT BOOKS
NEW YORK

CLB 874
© 1988 Colour Library Books Ltd, Godalming, Surrey, England.
All rights reserved.
This 1991 edition published by Crescent Books,
distributed by Outlet Book Company, Inc, a Random House Company,
225 Park Avenue South, New York, New York 10003.
Text filmsetting by Acesetters Ltd, Richmond, Surrey, England.
Printed in Hong Kong.
ISBN 0 517 47789 0
8 7 6 5 4 3 2

Except for the Pacific Northwest, no place in the United States gets more rainfall than the section of the southern Appalachian Mountains that straddles the border of North Carolina and Tennessee known as the Great Smoky Mountains. The result is lush forests, rushing streams and natural springs, which one mountain man says provides "the finest water in this world – clear and sweet year 'round and three degrees colder than ice."

The first people to live there were the Cherokee, whose descendants still live there. Though the mountains were very much a part of their lives, they lived at the edge of them. One of their strongest legends told them that the mountains themselves were inhabited by a race of tiny men, not at all unlike elves or leprechauns, who were quite friendly but who thought it was great fun to lead strangers into mountain glens and get them lost.

White men didn't get serious about settling the Smokies until after 1800. The 5,000-foot crest of the mountains made them easier to go around than through and besides, what if there really were little people up there?

The people who finally did take a chance were what American historians call "Scotch-Irish." They were the sons and daughters of a group of Scottish Presbyterians who were banished from their homes and went to Northern Ireland at about the same time the Puritans left for New England. Discrimination followed them to Ireland and they followed the lead of the Pilgrims, winding up in Delaware and Pennsylvania. High land prices there pushed them south, and by the beginning of the 19th century they had pushed to the highlands, the Great Smoky Mountains, which to them in many ways was like the land of their ancestors.

Once they found it, time stopped. They lived their lives and raised their children in relative isolation. Descendants of original families with names like Oliver and Shields, Caldwell, Sutton and Sherrill live in towns with names like Cade's Cove, Greenbriar, Pigeon Forge and Meig's Post. Their grandfathers remember the great religious revivals of the early 19th century that included such things as snake-handling, speaking in "tongues" and falling victim to "the jerks," an affirmation of accepting religion through exhausting body motions. Their fathers probably went to school in log cabins or learned to read the Bible or "Pilgrim's Progress" at their mothers' knees.

Progress came to the Smokies, as it came to many other parts of the country, in the years between the two World Wars. Because they lived off the land and had little other industry besides logging, the people of the Smokies weren't affected by the Great Depression as much as other Americans. But the automobile was beginning to bring the outside world in, and the money many received in lumbering made them want to see what that outside world might be like.

As early as 1920, there was a solid movement to establish a National Park in the Southern Mountains. But there were thousands of landowners to be dealt with. Private groups raised $1 million to do the job, but it wasn't nearly enough. Then, in 1926, the Governments of Tennessee and North Carolina added another $4 million and two years later John D. Rockefeller, Jr. doubled the nest egg.

It wasn't quite all they needed, but the Federal Government raised the total to $12 million in 1933 and the Great Smoky Mountains National Park became an attainable goal.

Improving the land became possible the same year through one of President Roosevelt's famous "New Deal" programs. It was the Civilian Conservation Corps which put young men to work, at $30 a month, all over the country in wilderness projects, flood control, conservation. It couldn't have come at a better time for the Smokies. Thousands of C.C.C. men went to work building roads and landscaping, improving trails, building bridges. The Park they built has been a joyous experience for millions since it was formally opened in 1940.

Though no two National Parks are exactly alike, The Great Smoky Mountains National Park is unique in not having moved all the people from their homes. Many previous owners of park land have opted to accept lifetime leases on their homes and to keep on working their fields. Their rustic cabins, their unique rail fences, their fascinating faces are as much an attraction to Park visitors as the bears and wild boars that still range in the interior.

Their tradition of handicrafts and mountain music are a lure, too. But most of all, it's the Smokies themselves that most people remember best. There is still an air of mystery about them, and the peaks and valleys the Cherokee sang about are still covered with the colors of sourwood trees and some 1200 species of flowering plants. And the contrasts of the hardwood forests with stands of balsam and spruce make even the most jaded of us feel like singing.

Facing page: landscape near Laurel Falls.

Facing page: (top) Lake Junaluska and (bottom) a small farm, both near Waynesville. Top and right: fine views of the foothills near Maggie Valley. Above: horses grazing near Cashiers.

5

Top: the West Carolina University Campus at Sylva. Left and above: a suspension footbridge near Sylva. Facing page: (top) river near Hartford and (bottom) hills near Big Witch Gap. Overleaf: views from the Blue Ridge Parkway.

Above: the Tuskegee Baptist Church.
Remaining pictures: the still waters of
Fontana Lake, an artificial body of
water contained by the tallest dam east
of the Rockies.

Top, left and facing page bottom: farmland near Cherokee. Above: gift shops on the outskirts of Cherokee. Facing page top: cloud-filled valleys near Birdtown.

Previous pages: (left) views from the
summit of Newfound Gap and (right) the
Oconaluftee River. Facing page top:
Mingus Mill. Facing page bottom and
this page: the nearby Pioneer
Farmstead. Overleaf: a view from the
Newfound Gap Road.

17

This page: the Observation Tower and view from Clingman's Dome. Facing page: scenes near Mount Collins. Overleaf: (top left) Observation Tower on Clingman's Dome; (bottom left) sunset near Newfound Gap; (top right) view from Clingman's Dome and (bottom right) nearby mountains.

Previous pages and left: rock-strewn
streams in the woodland near Chimney
Tops (top). Above: LaConte Creek.
Facing page: (top) a black bear and
(bottom) the view from Chimney Tops.

Previous pages: views from the Morton
Overlook. This page and overleaf:
scenes along the Roaring Fork Motor
Nature Trail. Facing page: (bottom)
scene near Alum Cave and (top) near
Grotto Falls.

Facing page: Rainbow Falls, near
Cherokee Orchard. Top: still waters at
Pittman. Above: autumn foliage near
Gatlinburg. Right: a stream near
Greenbrier. Overleaf: a boulder-strewn
stream near Greenbrier.

Previous pages: scenes near Pitman. Top and facing page bottom: the popular resort town of Gatlinburg, which caters for many of the visitors to Smoky Mountains National Park. Left: the Little Pigeon River. Above: Pigeon Forge. Facing page top: the Dollywood Theme Park, Pigeon Forge. Overleaf: the Old Mill at Pigeon Forge.

These pages: Gatlinburg. Facing page: (top) the Village, a downtown shopping mall, and (bottom) the Space Needle. Above: the Ober Gatlinburg Aerial Tramway. Top and right: the Sky Lift on Crockett Mountain. Overleaf: the Little River. Following pages: Laurel Falls.

Previous pages: (top left) the trail to
Laurel Falls; (bottom left) the view
from Maloney Point; (top right) a scene
near Clingman's Dome and (bottom right)
Little River. Facing page: a stream at
Metcalf Bottoms. This page: scenes
along the Little River Road. Overleaf:
woodland near Laurel Falls.

When the Great Smoky Mountains National Park was created, it was found that many old buildings still stood at Cades Cove (these pages) and they have now been restored and preserved. Overleaf: the Little River at Metcalf Bottoms.

Top: tobacco leaves drying in the Wear
Valley. Above: the Tuckalechee Caverns,
Townsend. Right: a church in the Wear
Valley. Facing page: (top) Cable Mill
and (bottom) farm buildings in the Wear
Valley. Overleaf: fall in the Great Smoky
Mountains National Park.